Praise

A great guide for anyone that is looking to knock their next interview out of the ballpark. Unlike other guides, this workbook provides you with a format where you *have to practice*. Even if you are fresh out of school or are looking to make a career change, this gives you the tools to present your best self…
— Kevin Carothers, CEO Visimar Design

I have interviewed many people in my career, and the Q&A portion of the interview seems to be difficult for even the most qualified candidates. This workbook would be a great tool to make anyone better at interviewing.
— Sue Bonar, Vice President of IBM Programs for Sirius Computer Solutions

No matter if you are starting your career, or if you are an experienced professional, the Powerhouse Interviewing Workbook provides an easy platform to prepare for an interview that will give you the confidence you need to land the job of your dreams.
— Marcus Melant, Chief Operating Officer of One World Touch

POWERHOUSE

"The First Interviewing Workbook That Provides a Powerful Interactive Platform On How To Present Your "Best Self".

• Gain Confidence & Understanding •

INTERViEWING
WORKBOOK

Mukta Lele Paliwal   Justin Jones

POWERHOUSE

TATE PUBLISHING & *Enterprises*

Powerhouse Interviewing Workbook
Copyright © 2009 by Mukta Paliwal and Justin Jones. All rights reserved.

No part of this publication may be reproduced, stored in a retrieval system or transmitted in any way by any means, electronic, mechanical, photocopy, recording or otherwise without the prior permission of the author except as provided by USA copyright law.

No part of this publication may be reproduced, stored in a retrieval system or transmitted in any way by any means, electronic, mechanical, photocopy, recording or otherwise without the prior permission of the author except as provided by USA copyright law.

The opinions expressed by the author are not necessarily those of Tate Publishing, LLC.

Published by Tate Publishing & Enterprises, LLC
127 E. Trade Center Terrace | Mustang, Oklahoma 73064 USA
1.888.361.9473 | www.tatepublishing.com

Tate Publishing is committed to excellence in the publishing industry. The company reflects the philosophy established by the founders, based on Psalm 68:11, *"The Lord gave the word and great was the company of those who published it."*

Book design copyright © 2009 by Tate Publishing, LLC. All rights reserved.
Cover design by Kandi Evans
Interior design by Lindsay B. Behrens
Caricatures by Chuck Brewer

Published in the United States of America
ISBN: 978-1-61566-476-4
1. Business & Economics / Careers / Job Hunting
2. Study Aids / Professional
09.11.23

Acknowledgment

I would like to give special thanks and all my love to Angela, Briggs, Urban, and all my family and great friends for their never-ending support.

—JJ

I would like to thank my husband, Sandeep, and my parents and friends for giving their support and the inspiration to make this happen.

—MLP

Caricatures by Chuck Brewer

Table of Contents

Introduction 11
Getting Started 15
Understanding the Q&A 19
General Interview Questions .27
Sales Interview Questions 115
Questions to Ask the Interviewer 169
Powerhouse Tips for a Successful Interview 173
The Brag Book 177
Plan Your Work, and Work Your Plan:
Powerhouse 30–60–90 Day Action Plan 181
Post-interviewing Information. 193

Introduction

Congratulations on taking the first step toward becoming a master at interviewing. Whether you are new or experienced with the interview process, this workbook will help you develop, practice, refine, and master your interviewing skills so you will *always* be presenting your best self in the interview.

Now that you have done your due diligence to get an interview, it's time to use this tool to ensure you are making the most of your opportunity. *Powerhouse Interviewing Workbook* will not only teach you about proper ways to present yourself and answer interview questions, but this one-of-a-kind workbook will allow you to customize and prepare yourself for *your* best interview. It doesn't matter whether you are new to the job market or a seasoned professional, interviewing for a job can be challenging and stressful. One thing we have found in our twenty-plus years of experience is that interviewing is a learned skill that requires preparation and *practice!* Using this workbook will provide you with the tools you need to present yourself in a relaxed and professional manner.

Powerhouse Interviewing Workbook begins with a brief overview of the information exchange process along with our method of answering questions. You are also provided with sample questions from which you can practice and sample responses for you to customize. To ensure that you have a reference scale, we have provided examples of responses to these questions. There are literally thousands of different questions that could be asked during an interview. We are going to focus on some of the most common ones. Remember, these questions may be asked in a variety of different ways. Reviewing the questions that we have provided and practicing how to answer them will help you prepare for any type of questions that might come up during an interview. We developed two sets of questions in this workbook: the first set is generalized, and the second set focuses on questions more commonly asked in sales interviews. It is important to review and practice all of the questions.

POWERHOUSE POINTER: No matter if your interviewing for a human resources, finance, customer service, engineering position, etc., your goal is to convince the interviewer that the skills and talents you bring to the table won't just be valuable to the position, but to the company as well.

Even though the Q&A (questions & answers) is the major focus of the interview, there are other facets that need to be considered, such as questions for the interviewer and correspondence letters. There is an additional section in *Powerhouse Interviewing Workbook* that provides you with examples of questions that you can ask the interviewer along with sample thank you letters. Other useful bits of wisdom referred to as "Powerhouse Pointer's" are placed throughout the text to provide additional tips and insight. "The Brag Book" and the "Powerhouse 30–60–90 Day Action Plan" are bonus features that are going to take you from an average candidate to an interviewing superstar. We have seen how effectively these items distinguish an individual in a competitive interviewing environment, and we know they can work for you.

After completing this workbook, you will have a practical understanding of how to effectively present yourself in a professional and compelling manner. This will ultimately give you the advantage over the competition and enable you to successfully navigate the interview process and land the job of your dreams.

POWERHOUSE POINTER: "People will forget what you said, people will forget what you did, but people will never forget how you made them feel" (Maya Angelou). The energy and passion you bring to an interview can be a major determining factor.

Getting Started

Before going into an interview, it is important to properly research and do your due diligence on the prospective company and the position or role you are seeking. Having background knowledge about the organization shows the employer how interested you are in the opportunity. Background knowledge on a company will also be beneficial in helping you formulate intelligent and appropriate answers and questions during the interview. One simple way company information can often be obtained is via the Internet. Your objective is to learn as much in-depth information as you can about the organization. Some topics to research are:

- What is the company culture like, and is it a good match for you?
- What are the goals of the company (short-term and long-term)?
- How do the company's products or services compare to the competition?

- What type of career growth can be expected from this position?
- What are the industry trends?
- What will your capacity be within the organization?
- Whom will you be working with, and whom will you be working for?

Once you think you have a good foundation of the prospective company and position, then you are halfway there. The next step is to talk to someone who can give you more in-depth information about the company. If you are going through a recruiter, don't hesitate to use them as a resource for company information. If you know anyone who works for the company, ask them for advice or tips to help you in the interview. Being able to consult someone on the inside is the best way you can prepare for an interview. You can find these people using networking contacts, through the internet, going through career centers or school alumni, and if those options don't work, go to the company to see if someone will meet with you. There is nothing wrong with showing your interest for a position with a company as long as you are not overly aggressive.

POWERHOUSE POINTER: The more you know about a company, the better off you will be. You can never know too much.

To help you get started, here is a quick list of Powerhouse Pre-interviewing tips:

1. Research the company you are interviewing before the interview.
2. Search the Web or read some trade journals to get a sense of the industry that you are interested in. What are the trends? What are some of the opportunities? What are some of the challenges?
3. Make sure your references know that you are interviewing and with whom you are interviewing. A surprise phone call does not always result in the best recommendation.
4. Map out the location of the interview and be prepared to arrive at least fifteen to twenty minutes early.
5. Do research on the competition. Understand the differences between products and services.
6. Have multiple clean copies of your résumé available.
7. Make sure your hair and nails are well groomed.
8. Dress appropriately. Formal business attire is the safest strategy for an interview.
9. Only bring what you need (résumés, brag book, etc.)
10. Turn your cell phone off or keep it on silent mode.
11. Get plenty of rest the night before.
12. If you have an ally at the company where you will be interviewing, let them know in advance when and with whom your interview is to see if they can give you any helpful advice or information.

13. Make sure you have *practiced, practiced, practiced* your responses for the sample interviewing questions.
14. Have a Powerhouse 30–60–90 Action Plan prepared to share during the interview.
15. Make sure your brag book is updated and organized to present.

POWERHOUSE POINTER: If you have a My Space, Facebook, Twitter, or any other type of social/networking account, make sure that there is not any inappropriate subject matter, pictures, or content. HR departments will search these sites during their background checks.

Understanding the Q&A

Hiring and training new employees has become an extremely time-consuming and costly endeavor. Employers are more rigorous than ever with their approach to the selection and hiring process. The Q&A segment of the interview has become one of the most valuable methods for enabling companies to make better decisions in choosing appropriate candidates. Interview questions are designed not only to prompt a discussion of your qualifications, but also to gain a deeper insight into your behavior and personality. This is known as behavioral interviewing.

Behavioral interviewing is a technique in which the questions asked assist the employer in evaluating a potential employee's future success based on past behaviors. This is based on the belief that past success is a good indicator of future performance. Unlike traditional interviews where the candidate may talk about hypothetical situations, these interviews deal with "real life" examples.

Even though it would seem that answering these questions should be fairly easy because they are about you, this part of the interview tends to be the most difficult for interviewees. In our twenty-plus years of experience, we have seen many great job candidates lose opportunities due to inadequate preparation or overconfidence in their ability to answer interview questions.

To maximize your effectiveness in the Q&A session, it is important to understand the simple psychology of the questions. Companies use the interviewing process to generally find out the answers to these questions:

- Will you take it upon yourself to manage your own development?
- How long will it take you to get acclimated and become productive in your position?
- Do you have potential to be a high performer in the company?
- Are you amiable and easy to work with?
- What type of results will you achieve in the position?
- Do you fit the company culture, is it a good match?
- Are you responsible and reliable?
- Do you need to be supervised, or are you self motivated?
- If you get the position, what would your longevity be with the company?

Knowing this provides guidance on what you need to convey in an interview. No question is difficult to answer when you are properly prepared. Understanding the interviewer's intent when you are asked the seemingly hard questions will lead to more appropriate answers.

The questions in this workbook were designed to help you formulate answers that highlight your capabilities and strengths. They are laid out in a simple format: the question, the thought process (the psychology behind the question), and the sample response. When you start to go through these sections, you will see that we have incorporated two sample responses when applicable to the question. One is directed toward an experienced professional, the other for a new professional, or the sample response will be for both if indicated. A new professional is someone we have classified as a recent college graduate or a person who is just starting their career. To make sure this workbook will help as many people as possible, we included the *new professional response* to provide an example of how to astutely answer interviewing questions with only having minimal or no professional experience in your background. The sample responses provided are merely examples of the many different ways there are to answer these questions. Whether you're an experienced or new professional, it would be advantageous to review all of the responses to help gain a broader understanding of how to effectively answer interviewing questions. As stated in the introduction, interviewing is a learned skill that takes preparation and practice. In both sections, there is space below each question for you to provide your own unique responses. Remember, you will need to add your own charming personality and professional/personal examples to the interview.

POWERHOUSE POINTER: In an interview, you don't necessarily have to have professional experience to prove to an employer that you can do the job. Draw similarities from experiences with your life or education that pertain to the questions that are being asked. Articulate your answers to convey *energy, desire,* and *willingness* to do whatever it takes to be successful.

To further assist with your efforts, we have designed an easy-to-use technique to answer interview questions in order to more effectively identify and describe your strengths and minimize your weaknesses in an interview. The Powerhouse Feature/Accomplishment/Benefit technique—*FAB* for short—is used for presenting your background and experience to an employer. The Powerhouse FAB technique does several important things: it highlights your unique features and experiences, it details what you have accomplished in your current and previous positions or from your education, and finally it shows specifically what you can do for the employer and how you will benefit him/her and the organization. If you are a new professional, you can use this technique to talk about organizations you belonged to, leadership roles you have held, part-time jobs, or experiences in your education that pertain to the position you are interviewing for. You can also speak to your college experience in terms of how you chose the school you attended, how you financed it, your work ethic, time management, and organizational skills that were involved.

POWERHOUSE POINTER: When using the Powerhouse FAB technique, try to deliver your message within sixty seconds or less to help maintain a good flow of dialogue between you and the interviewer.

How do you prepare a Powerhouse FAB response? Start by defining some terms:

Features—Facts about yourself; description of a situation in which you had to demonstrate the use of a unique feature or strength that pertain to the question.

Accomplishments—Significant, measurable results you obtained for your current and past employers, or in school. Discuss how you used the feature or strength and what actions you took to achieve the result.

Benefits—Describe how these accomplishments can translate into what you can do for a new employer.

Research has shown that there is a big difference between what a person thinks he or she will say and what is actually said. This is why it is important to formulate your responses to the questions first and then practice verbalizing them. It is a great idea to enlist the help of a trusted friend or family member and practice your interview techniques and presentation skills. It is also helpful to stand in front of a mirror and watch yourself verbalize your responses. This gives you an opportunity to observe your facial expressions and body language while speaking. You may also find it beneficial to record yourself speaking out your responses. This can help you not only modify your tone and speed, but also improve the quality of your answers.

 **POWERHOUSE POINTER:** Non-verbal language can be more powerful than your spoken words. Use good posture and eye contact, and watch out for shrewd facial expressions. Smile!

Interviewing Workbook 23

As you go through the workbook, you will notice there are two separate sets of questions. The first set consists of general interview questions. These questions are not specific to any particular job, career, or industry. The second set of questions is specifically for a sales interview. We thought it was important to include sales-specific questions because sales is the number-one occupation and the questions associated with a sales interview tend to be more unique. Both sets of questions are designed to allow the interviewer to learn more about your background, experiences, skills you possess, how you handle certain situations, the type of person you are, and what you bring to the table for the position.

Regardless of the position you are interviewing for, it would be in your best interest to review both sets of questions. Within any working environment you are always selling something, whether it's a concept or idea to your manager, a suggestion to a co-worker or subordinate, or a product or service to a customer, sales is embedded in everyone's job. Approaching most interviews from a sales angle can distinguish you from other candidates. Even if you are not interviewing for a sales position, these examples provide a great review to help you formulate new ideas for better responses to any type of interviewing questions. You may even read something in these sample responses that can be applied more specifically to your needs.

POWERHOUSE POINTER: The goal of every interview is to sell yourself to a potential employer.

Keep in mind that this interview is about you. Our purpose is to help you be well prepared so you present your *best* self. The information provided should help you expand your train of thought to more effectively communicate well-formed answers to tough questions.

POWERHOUSE POINTER: It is important to understand there are many ways to ask the same question. Don't get thrown off if you don't hear a question asked like it is presented in this workbook. Pay attention to the question and take a second to formulate your response. The more time you take practicing responses to questions in this book, the better prepared you'll be for any type of questions you might face in an interview.

General Interview Questions

1. Why are you interested in the position?

Thought process:
The interviewer is looking at your interest level and knowledge of the position. She wants to see if you have done your homework and have an understanding of what the position entails. She wants to make sure that you are aware of the challenges involved in the position. She is also attempting to determine your motivation for seeking this specific position.

Sample response:
I am interested in the position because I am interested in a career with your organization. Briggs Logistics is a very well respected transportation company that has been listed as one of the top Fortune 500 companies to work for. I like being in human resources and have a proven track record. I understand that the position requires organization, good communication skills, and a team-focused attitude, which I have demonstrated in my past

experience. This position also provides a great opportunity to work with other departments within the company, which is very exciting to me. I am looking for a career and not a job, and the challenges of this position appeal to me.

New professional response:
I graduated with a degree in finance, and I know this is the field I want to have a career in. Urban Investments is a very well respected investment firm that has had steady growth in the past ten years, and I believe this is a company where I can grow my career long term. I understand that the position requires organization, good communication skills, and a team-focused attitude. These are traits that I possess, and I believe I would be a great fit with Urban Investments.

POWERHOUSE POINTER: Before you interview for a specific job, make a list of the characteristics that are important to you. Do your research so that you are well prepared. Job descriptions have good information that you must use when answering questions. For example, if the job description asks for organizational skills, use the term "organizational skills" in your response and demonstrate with one or two specific examples. Here are some topics that could be included in your response if they apply to you:

1. cutting-edge industry
2. challenging environment
3. interest in (the industry)
4. ever-changing, new products; mentally stimulating

Your unique response:

_____

_____

_____

_____

_____

_____

_____

2. Why are you specifically interested in LeLe Computer Inc.? What do you know about our products?

Thought process:
Again, the interviewer wants to see if you have done your homework on the company and the products or services. This question is more specific than the previous one. He is assessing your understanding of the industry and the company's products. The interviewer wants to know that you are making a well-thought-out career move. Answering the question thoroughly demonstrates to the manager that you have made the effort to learn about his company and are not scrambling to get a job—any job.

Sample response for both experienced and new professionals:
After much research on the industry, I have taken an interest in your company because you are the leader in innovative computer products. LeLe Computer Inc. has an outstanding track record in innovation and customer service. Your new computer processor is a very unique product that fits a niche in the market that no one else can fill. I really like how LeLe Computer Inc. understands the needs of the consumer, and I would like to be part of an exciting place like LeLe Computer Inc.

POWERHOUSE POINTER: Do your homework by talking to current employees and customers to find out about the culture of the company, issues that are being faced, and possible solutions. Be sure to demonstrate this knowledge in your interview.

Your unique response:

3. What drives you?

Thought process:
The interviewer is looking for an individual who demonstrates high standards. She is also trying to assess how you are motivated. Bottom line, the interviewer is looking for the "can do" attitude.

Sample response:
What drives me is an environment where I am rewarded for my competitive and winning nature. I like to be part of a team but also to be recognized for "thinking outside the box" and developing unique strategies that benefit the company and the customers. For example, I was part of an internal project team that was transitioning our accounts-payable department over to a new software platform. I was the team leader and had been asked to complete this transition in a very short period of time. Since I enjoy being able to complete projects before deadlines, I was able to complete the transition in three weeks instead of four, saving the company an additional week of possible downtime and a lot of money. My team and I were not only recognized for the speed and accuracy with which we finished the project but also given a monetary bonus for the achievement.

New professional response:
I am a very results driven person and enjoy taking on new challenges and figuring out solutions. I served two years as the fundraising chairperson for the Hispanic Society in school. I was challenged constantly to come up with new ideas to raise money for our non-profit organization. While in this role, I created three new annual benefits that have helped the society raise record amounts in donations.

 **POWERHOUSE POINTER:** Answer each question with a specific example that helps paint the picture of what you will bring to the table and how it relates to the position. Remember to listen to the questions, clarify, and then answer. Remember also to state your answer in measurable terms, as the interviewee above did in giving the number of weeks it took to complete the transition.

Your unique response:

4. Which personality profile describes you? Driven, amiable, expressive, or analytical? Is there a certain personality type you find difficult to work for or with?

Thought process:
This is a dual question that leads to more insight about you and how you work with others. The interviewer is looking for your understanding of the different personality types and your ability to adapt to each style with positive results. Be sure to let your personality come through when answering this question.

Sample response:
I am amiable in the sense that I am able to work with all different personality types and enjoy it. I think this is a key to my success. I also see some of the "driven" traits in me. I set goals for myself with timelines. For example, in my first job which I started in the mailroom, I made it a goal that at the end of three months I would know everyone in our office, including their names and job titles. The personality type I find the most difficult to work with is an apathetic person. This is a tough personality type because regardless of what you do with them, they do not care, and they are very difficult to impact.

New professional response:
I would say I am a driven person. If I am given a task or a project, I don't need someone to push me to get it finished. I pride myself in taking things head-on; of course I'm not afraid to ask for help or assistance if I need it. This helped me stay on track in school with the projects and written assignments I was responsible for. The personality type I find the most difficult to work with is an apathetic person. This is a tough personality type because regardless of what you do with them, they do not care, and they are very difficult to impact.

**POWERHOUSE POINTER:** Interviews are meant to capture the total essence of what a person will bring to a company. You have to be able to handle the position, but there are other variables such as personality and ability to work with others that are also important. Developing chemistry is vital during the interview.

Your unique response:

_____

_____

_____

_____

_____

_____

_____

_____

5. What do you value more: team or individual success?

Thought process:
The interviewer is looking for your ability to work as an individual but also wants to see your ability to work within a group to reach a common goal. You must be strong in both areas. Remember, no one wants someone they have to babysit or someone who will not help the overall company objective.

Sample response:
For most of my career I have worked with or led teams. What I have been able to do is effectively delegate various tasks so that everyone has ownership for specific aspects of the project. This way everyone can see their contributions. This also allows for is individual creativity. When you collect all the pieces together, it is a winning formula. I like knowing that I am able to contribute to the overall success of a team as an individual. Seeing the success of a team project that is due to the many individual coordinated efforts is very rewarding to me.

New professional response:
While attending school, I had the opportunity to work on both individual projects and group projects. They each provided their own challenges and rewards. With an individual project, I didn't have to worry about someone else doing their part, but everything was on my shoulders. In a group, different parts of the project could be divided up, but then you had to make sure everyone did their share. I like individual projects and knowing that they are accomplished by my efforts alone, but I also liked the experiences shared by working together as team to accomplish a goal. I see the value and importance of both.

 **POWERHOUSE POINTER:** When interviewing, provide examples of times you achieved individual success or group success. Be able to show that you can be successful and productive either way.

Your unique response:

6. Have you ever been part of a group where your ideas were not supported?

Thought process:
The interviewer is looking for your ability to gauge and work within a group dynamic. He wants to see your negotiating skills and how you handle conflict. He wants the assurance that you do not receive the rejection of your ideas or suggestions personally, but you are able to remain calm and negotiate your way through it. Think: situation, action, outcome.

Sample response:
I was involved in a group that was creating and designing marketing plans for new territories. I presented several ideas that were not enthusiastically received by my peers. I calmly and empathetically listened to what they felt would be effective. I then discussed the benefits of the ideas I had presented and how combining some of their ideas with my own would be of greatest benefit. This approach gained support, and we were able to complete the marketing plan for the new territories.
*Note: If something like this response is your example, be prepared to explain the idea.

New professional response:
I have been a part of many teams, organizations, or groups working on a project, and there have been times that my ideas were not supported. If I truly believe in an idea, then I will present a case for it. If my idea doesn't get accepted, I don't take it personally. I just want what is best for the group.

 **POWERHOUSE POINTER:** Conflict resolution is a skill that is valuable not only when dealing with groups from your organization, but also in diffusing situations when a customer is unhappy with your product or service. Try to include examples of your ability to resolve conflict in your interview.

Your unique response:

_____

_____

_____

_____

_____

_____

_____

_____

7. Tell me how you had to modify your behavior with a person in order to accomplish a goal.

Thought process:
The interviewer is looking for personal flexibility to attain a common goal. She is looking for your ability to adjust your interaction style as needed to work with different personalities. Sacrificing morals is not acceptable behavior modification.

Sample response:
I believe that everyone is unique. By this I mean personality, drive, beliefs, etc. I try to adjust my communication and mannerism style for the individual with whom I'm working. I have found that this is the most effective way to get a point across or to accomplish a goal in business or everyday life. For example, there was a time when I was working closely with a very process-oriented individual. When I began working with him, I realized that my flowery, expressive language was not getting my point across. As a consequence, in the beginning we missed a few deadlines. When I realized how this individual approached his work, I changed my approach and submitted ideas in flowcharts and process diagrams. Not only did we make deadlines after that, but we were able to collaborate on other projects that contributed to the growth of our department revenues by 10 percent.

New professional response:
I believe that everyone is unique. By this I mean personality, drive, beliefs, etc. I try to adjust my communication and mannerism style for the individual with whom I'm working. I have found that this is the most effective way to get a point across or to accomplish a goal in everyday life. For example, I was partnered with a classmate of

mine to work on an in-class assignment for Business Management. We had two hours to come up with an innovative business idea and an example of how we would market it. My partner was hyper, not focused, and wanted to talk about everything but our assignment. Instead of getting frustrated with her, I made a comment about her great energy and asked if she could use that to help us come up with a cool idea. I was able to get her focused, and we had one of the most interesting concepts in the class.

 **POWERHOUSE POINTER:** "The art of life is a constant readjustment to our surroundings" (Kakuzo Okakaura).

Your unique response:

8. Describe a situation where there was a disagreement and you had to resolve the problem.

Thought process:
The interviewer is looking your ability to negotiate, find common ground, and deliver a solution. He wants to see how you rationally overcome this type of adversity. Describe an example discussing these different points of negotiating.

Sample response:
In a district meeting with my manager and peers, we had a finite entertainment fund, and I had to decide how we were going to divide the money. The meeting got pretty emotional because some of my peers felt they deserved more funding than others. First, I listened to everyone's opinion with an open mind. I then suggested that we come up with an objective set of standards on which to base our funding distribution. We all brainstormed and eventually agreed to base our distribution on account potential, underperforming accounts, and accounts that would be impacted by entertaining. Based on this, we divided the funding up in a fair way. Not everyone was happy, but all agreed this was the best way to do it.

New professional response:
I worked part-time at JJ's Diner to help pay for school. One of my responsibilities was to make the weekly shift schedules for the wait staff. It was the week of Thanksgiving, and no one wanted to work Thanksgiving evening because it was slow. I knew I had to be fair about how I chose which servers to schedule, so I came up with the idea to give prime time shifts for three weeks to anyone who would volunteer that evening. I ended up having so many volunteers that I had to turn people away.

 **POWERHOUSE POINTER:** Successful decisions do not necessarily mean that everyone will be happy, but it does mean that there is consensus that it is the best way to proceed.

Your unique response:

_____
_____
_____
_____
_____
_____
_____
_____
_____

9. Who do you consider a mentor in your life? Who has had the most influence on your life and why? How would this person describe you?

Thought process:
The interviewer is looking to see what person helped shape you into the person you are today. Think of the big three: professional skills, personal skills, and work ethic. Just make sure your mentor is worth emulating. Provide a specific example of what they taught you and how it has translated into a behavior in your life.

Sample response:
I would have to say my former manager. This person taught me the value of a strong work ethic, integrity, loyalty, and competitiveness. She showed me that what I might have lacked in experience, I could make up by working harder than everyone else. I also learned how important it is to be honest with the people you work with and to not be afraid to ask for help. She also taught me the value of helping others when they come to you. I would say she'd describe me as hard working, honest, and helpful.

New professional response:
During an internship with Briggs Petroleum, I got to work under the Project Manager for the Gulf Coast. I was able to learn and evaluate how he communicated with people, used different management styles, and organized his day to be as efficient as possible. He always said, "It's not how hard you work, it's how smart you work." The Project Manager would describe me as earnest and tenacious.

 **POWERHOUSE POINTER:** As you go through your professional life, it is a good idea to maintain an updated list of your work-related mentors and what they have taught you. This is part of your professional development.

Your unique response:

_____

_____

_____

_____

_____

_____

_____

_____

10. How do you keep up with current events?

Thought process:
The interviewer is looking for a well-rounded person. You either keep up with events, or you do not. If you do not normally keep up with current events, start doing it now. Your answer also provides some insight about you as a person and what interests you have.

Sample response:
I usually check the newspaper and the Internet. I also listen to news on the radio while I am driving. I have a subscription to trade journals to keep abreast of trends and news in the industry. Another activity that keeps me "plugged in" is being part of a networking group, which has allowed me to grow professionally as well as increase my knowledge of the industry.

New professional response:
I usually check out major news updates on the Internet. As a member of the Hospitality Society in college, we met weekly to discuss changes and new trends in the restaurant and hotel industry. I joined other groups on campus that were aligned with the industries I wanted to be a part of to increase my networking once I completed my degree. I think it would be difficult to be successful if you didn't stay up to date on new information in your industry.

POWERHOUSE POINTER: Take the time each day, maybe fifteen to thirty minutes, to update yourself via the Web, newspaper, magazines, etc. Join local networking groups for your specific area of interest or area you are interested in being part of in the future. Being up-to-date on current events/people is a great way to enhance your small talk discussions and make yourself more successful.

Your unique response:

_____

_____

_____

_____

_____

_____

_____

_____

11. Tell us about yourself starting from high school (or college, depending on work history). Your presentation should include extra-curricular activities, work history, and so forth.

Thought process:
The interviewer wants to get to know you on a more personal level and have a better understanding of the path that led you to where you are today. Discuss key highlights that demonstrate leadership, drive, organization, success, responsibility, and goals you have set for yourself.

Sample response for both experienced and new professionals:
This is an absolutely unique answer for everyone, so we have provided some tips to help you write your own response.

Your presentation should be very structured. It should have a beginning, middle, and end. Talk about your interests and the decisions you made that led to your career path. Highlight any achievements along the way. Note any highlights in your high school/college/early career. Talk about how you decided to go to the college you attended (show some of your thought process) and any accomplishments. Mention organizations, clubs, or teams you were a member of. If you are an experienced professional, talk about your professional accomplishments. Be able to talk about this in three minutes and be prepared to be stopped and questioned along the way.

POWERHOUSE POINTER: Make your story so that it would be interesting to a class of tenth graders. They are a tough audience; if you can appeal to them, you can appeal to anyone.

Your unique response:

12. What do you consider your greatest accomplishment and why?

Thought process:
The interviewer wants to understand what you consider to be a significant accomplishment and why it is important to you. This also gives the interviewer some more in-depth insight to your background. Feel free to speak about anything in your life or professional career.

Sample response:
I was asked to work on a proposal with a previous company, and my team was on a strict timeline to get this completed. Even though it initially seemed impossible, I managed to lead the group, put in extra hours, and deliver it successfully on time. My company at the time only employed thirty people. We were competing with multinational companies who had staffs of thousands for this large project with international exposure. That is why when we won the bid and got the project, I felt like it was my greatest accomplishment. I was recognized for my effort and commitment to the project.

New professional response:
I graduated college with a 3.8 GPA. This is a major accomplishment in my life. I worked extremely hard, stayed focus, and achieved my goal of graduating with over 3.5 GPA. This proved to me that if I try hard and put in the effort, I can accomplish my goals. I feel confident that if given the opportunity, I can be successful at anything I do.

 **POWERHOUSE POINTER:** Your accomplishment should be a proud moment. Show your pride when you are communicating with the interviewer.

Your unique response:

_____

_____

_____

_____

_____

_____

_____

_____

_____

13. How do you measure success?

Thought process:
The interviewer wants to know what your definition of success is and whether it will match the company's. Speak of how you define success. Try to provide objective measures that translate into your professional life. Remember to show how your success not only benefitted you, but helped the company or others be successful.

Sample response:
I measure success by first defining goals. I set both short- and long-term goals and then cross-reference these with the expectations of my manager. I make sure that my goals are measurable and quantifiable. I always like to challenge myself both professionally and personally. For example, when I was hired in my previous position as staff accountant manager, I had been told that no one had been able to stay in the job for more than six months. I decided that part of defining success in this position would be not only to last longer than six months but also to turn the entire department around and significantly reduce turnover. I have been in this position for two years. I was promoted after my first year and have since promoted three people under me to team leaders. I think of this as being successful.

New professional response:
Success is defined as the achievement of something planned or attempted. I measure success by the accomplishment of short-term and long-term goals I have set for myself. I had to work part-time to support myself while going to school. I wasn't always able to take a full course load every semester, so I wasn't

able to graduate in four years. I made the goal for myself to graduate in five years. I made sure that I achieved my goal, and I did. This was a great success and achievement for me.

 **POWERHOUSE POINTER:** There is no point in taking a job that is not going to lead you to where you want to go the way you want to get there.

Your unique response:

_____

_____

_____

_____

_____

_____

_____

_____

14. What are your goals? Short range? Long range? How can our company help you fulfill those objectives?

Thought process:
The interviewer is trying to see whether you have planning capabilities and how you approach your career. He is also trying to understand how you view his organization as part of your future goals and wants to make sure the company can offer what you are looking for in a career. Make sure to clearly define goals you have set for yourself and be able to explain why you set those particular goals.

Sample response:
My short-term objective is to learn the ins and outs of customer service management and to be considered an expert in my position. Long-term I would like to take this experience and be involved in the planning and development of an international launch. Jones, Inc. is the market leader in making recycling a viable alternative for the clothing industry. I feel confident that I can contribute to the success of the company long-term. Since Jones, Inc. is a recognized leader in this product category globally, it will provide me with the long-term challenge that I am looking for.

New professional response:
Tournant, LLC is known for creating unique specialty products. My short-term goal is to learn and excel in the position of a customer service representative. Long-term, I would like to learn different aspects of the business and be able to use my creativity to help in the creation of a new product.

 **POWERHOUSE POINTER:** "A goal without a plan is just a wish" (Antoine De Saint Exupery).

Your unique response:

_____

_____

_____

_____

_____

_____

_____

_____

15. What was a difficult problem that you had to overcome, and how did you go about doing it?

Thought process:
The interviewer is trying to gauge what you view as a challenge. She is trying to determine whether what you view as a tremendous challenge is truly a challenge or just an inconvenience. She also wants to see how you handle adversity and formulate a solution to the problem.

Sample response:
One of the greatest problems we had at my company is shipping parts with zero percent breakage. We were getting a lot of complaints from our customers that the products they received were broken and had to be sent back. The customers' work was slowed down as a result. This went on for about two months. After careful investigation, I uncovered that our shipping containers were not suitable for the parts we were shipping. Once I identified the problem, we developed a better shipping container. Our customers were very happy, and complaints were significantly reduced.

New professional response:
A difficult problem I had to overcome was financing my education. I was able to get into a top university, but my financial assistance only partially covered my expenses. I was committed to my education and applied for grants and worked part time. This allowed me to pay for my schooling at a top university despite my humble background.

 **POWERHOUSE POINTER:** It is always good to keep a current list of professional challenges that you have faced and how you have overcome them. Consider keeping a journal; it is often hard to recall specifics unless you write them down.

Your unique response:

_____

_____

_____

_____

_____

_____

_____

_____

16. Why should we hire you?

Thought process:
The manager is looking for a professional to take on this opportunity. Make a convincing statement of why he should choose you over another candidate. He should see your confidence and your desire for the position. This is not the time to be humble.

Sample response:
I have a proven track record of success with multiple brands in more than one market segment. (Provide documented examples of any success you have had in your career. This is an opportunity to use your Brag Book) My long-term track record is impeccable, and I feel that my personality and the culture of your organization are an excellent match. Based on what I have shared with you, is there anything in my background that would preclude me from being considered?

New professional response:
I feel that my personality and the culture of your organization are an excellent match. I have held multiple leadership roles with different clubs and organizations throughout my college career. I pride myself in having a strong work ethic and desire to be successful. I am willing to do whatever it takes to become a contributing member to your team.

 **POWERHOUSE POINTER:** In the answering process, plan and think in terms of your own strengths and how they can translate into what the interviewer/organization needs are. Here are some common topics that could be included in your response if they apply to you:

1. build long-term relationships
2. interest in (the industry)
3. competitiveness to be the best
4. serve as a consultant to customers and provide additional value
5. proven team player

Your unique response:

_____

_____

_____

_____

_____

_____

_____

17. Give me an example of a high-pressure situation you have been under recently.

Thought process:
The interviewer is looking for your trigger points, threshold of patience, and the result of your frustration. She wants to determine how and where you direct your frustration. No one wants to hire a short-tempered loose cannon who would present the company in a negative light or be a challenge to work with and manage. Make sure to discuss the outcome of your actions.

Sample response:
One time I had an upset customer who did not understand a billing issue and called my supervisor without calling me first. This resulted in a meeting with my vice president to investigate why this customer was so upset. This customer did not realize how much we as an organization were doing for him. We were providing services above and beyond what a customer in his category would traditionally get. I was told that if we were not able to rectify the situation we would be jeopardizing other business. I set up a meeting to gain a better understanding of what the customer was angry about. I realized that it was a simple case of miscommunication. Finance had sent him a bill before the goods had even been delivered. (They were in transit.) He believed this implied that he couldn't be trusted to make payments. After speaking to him, I was able to clear up the miscommunication. The outcome resulted in the customer realizing the extent of our commitment to his company. He then apologized for his behavior, and now we have an even stronger relationship that has resulted in new business.

New professional response:
I was working part-time as the night shift assistant hotel manager when, due to the bad weather, the power went out. We had hundreds of worried guests that I was responsible for. I had to make sure that people with medical needs, disabilities, and young children were properly taken care of. We had a customer that required refrigeration for his medicine. I took it upon myself to drive in the bad weather and get him ice and an ice chest to store his medicine. The power eventually came back on, and all of the guests were extremely grateful for how we handled the situation.

POWERHOUSE POINTER: We all get frustrated, but how you handle your frustration is what is important. Maintaining professionalism is of utmost importance.

Your unique response:

_____

_____

_____

_____

_____

_____

_____

18. What are some of the obstacles you have had to overcome in your current position? (If you are a new professional, the interviewer will ask you about any situation where you had to overcome obstacles)

Thought process:
The interviewer realizes that everybody has obstacles to overcome. She is trying to determine how you perceive obstacles. Do you view them as a temporary challenge? Can you strategically think outside the box to overcome them? This is an opportunity to show how you think on your feet and how tenacious you are to overcome a challenge.

Sample response:
My company recently did a product recall. This was a tremendous challenge because the person who would have traditionally been in charge had just retired. The problem was passed on to me, and I was asked to lead the team that was responsible for replacing all the recalled products. I worked with the team to plan a strategy and timeline to notify all of the major accounts. We then proceeded to notify all of the smaller accounts in a timely fashion, providing them with an update regarding the product recall. We not only retained all our customers but were able to successfully switch them to another product that we offer.

New professional response:
In my position as an alumni liaison I had to overcome a tremendous bias from contributors due to my youth. I had to work extra hard to gain respect from donors. Once I was able to establish rapport, I was able to explain why we needed funds and how the funds were being used. Due to my persistence and ability to establish rapport I was the top fundraiser for the association last year.

 **POWERHOUSE POINTER:** Don't discuss the obstacle in a negative light, but use this question to show how you turned it into an opportunity.

Your unique response:

___

___

___

___

___

___

___

19. Tell me about a situation when you gave it your all; were not successful.

Thought process:
The interviewer is looking for tenacity and emotional resilience after a defeat. We have all suffered setbacks at one time or another. The interviewer wants to understand what you learned from the situation and how you are applying it to your career.

Sample response:
I was selling capital equipment to a municipal district. During my first year, I had the opportunity to try and win one of the largest accounts in my area. I put numerous hours into demonstrating my products and creating the proposal. I worked on the proposal during all my spare time. When it was time to present the bid, they loved my product and agreed it best met their needs. However, the account had a tight budget and was forced to buy the less expensive competitive product. Instead of looking at it as a loss, I continued to maintain my relationship with the municipal district. As a new year came up, they obtained increased funding. We rebid for the project, and this time my product was selected. I learned that even if at first pass things don't go your way, that does not mean that you will not reap the benefits in the long-term.

New professional response:
I was recently in a high-pressure situation with the "University Business Challenge." There were eight teams competing for the first prize of $10K. We were asked to develop a product and the entire marketing plan in ten days for a toy company. The judges were business executives from companies based locally, which

doubled the pressure. The strong desire to win the prize and to impress the judges (in case a career option opened up) created a tense situation. My team and I approached this methodically by working with everyone's strengths on the team. We were able to complete the project, but came in 2nd place. The contest was still a great opportunity and valuable experience.

 **POWERHOUSE POINTER:** A positive attitude and tenacity are traits that successful people possess.

Your unique response:

_____

_____

_____

_____

_____

_____

_____

_____

20. What do you do when your schedule has to be altered?

Thought process:
The interviewer is looking for your ability to handle change and stress. He is also determining how you set priorities. The manager wants to ensure that you are not fazed by a sudden change in your plans. He wants to know if you stay calm and turn the change into an opportunity, or does it negatively impact you?

Sample response:
I had a client that had an emergency and needed to change his appointment with me (his company's network went down). I had been waiting six months to get this appointment. I was calm and patient and rescheduled the appointment. I used the time for paperwork and planning for future business opportunities. I was also able to find out some additional information from the secretary that better prepared me for my future appointment.

New professional response:
This is something that happens with so many things in life. I have had classes cancelled at the last minute. When that has happened, I have utilized that time to catch up on my studying and research projects. I believe that I am a flexible person and I am able to make adjustments fairly easy.

POWERHOUSE POINTER: Just because an appointment is cancelled doesn't mean that it is wasted time in your schedule. Utilize that time to help you either catch-up or get ahead with other work.

Your unique response:

21. What is the most significant contribution you have made to your employer?

Thought process:
The interviewer is attempting to assess the unique qualities you would bring to the company. He also wants to find out more about what you accomplished with your previous company and how those skills or experiences will translate into the new position.

Sample response:
I feel the most significant contribution I made to my company was developing professional business relationships and reducing internal turnover. Before I came on board, the turnover was close to 38 percent. Since I have been working with my current company as manager of human resources, turnover has dropped to 20 percent. The increased tenure of our employees has resulted in better professional relationships and, as a consequence, increased business.

POWERHOUSE POINTER: What you might perceive as inconsequential could be quite impressive to someone else. Don't sell yourself short.

Your unique response:

22. Tell me about your last manager. (These can all be tied in with this question.) Did you like him/her? If I were your manager, what would be the best way to coach you to success? What qualities should a successful manager possess? Describe the relationship that should exist between the supervisor and those reporting to him or her. For a new professional, this question might simply be referenced toward qualities you would like in a manager.

Thought process:
The hiring manager is looking to see if she can work with you. The interviewer is also looking at your perception of authority, your willingness to learn, how you handle criticism, and how you like to be managed. The interviewer needs to understand what support to provide and what tools you may need to be successful. The relationship between a manager and employee should be open, honest, encouraging, and accountable on both sides. Be careful how you answer this question. Again, no manager bashing allowed!

Sample response:
I liked my manager, and we had a positive working relationship. We had similar thought processes on the objectives of my position and how to best manage me, which was to give me all the tools (training, funding) necessary to be successful and then let me work my position in a way to exceed expectations. I would like a manager who periodically offers advice and suggestions for improvement and who also provides open, constructive criticism. I feel the most important qualities of a successful manager are as follows: high expectations, openness, honesty, excellent communication skills, and the ability to assist me in my career development and goal attainment. I want an open and candid relationship with my manager.

 **POWERHOUSE POINTER:** Choose your examples carefully. The examples used in your responses can say a lot about how you would approach a situation. Focusing on what has worked in the past to make you successful helps the interviewer think about how you would fit in to their organization.

Your unique response:

_____

_____

_____

_____

_____

_____

_____

_____

23. Tell me about a setback in your career or in your life.

Thought process:
The interviewer is looking for resilience, open mindedness, and flexibility. The interviewer is also looking for an optimistic, upbeat perspective on a difficult situation and how you overcame the difficulty.

Sample response:
I was working my way up with a company, and just when I was about to see the fruit of my labor, the company was bought out. I was given the opportunity to take a position with the acquiring organization. Unfortunately, this put me in a situation where I was going to have to start all over again. Even though this was a setback, I took the experience I had gained in my career and put it to use with a new company and I was able to get back on track toward my career goals.

New professional response:
A setback for me happened while I was in school. I had to deal with my financial assistance being cut off due to the downturn in the economy. I went to the financial assistance office and to my advisor to see what my options were. By networking and being persistent I was able to get a teaching assistant position in the physics department. I was able to use those funds to help contribute towards the cost of my education.

 **POWERHOUSE POINTER:** "Our greatest glory is not in never falling but in rising every time we fall" (Confucius). Never say, "I have not suffered any setbacks." Think about any challenging situation that required extra effort and know-how. The interviewer wants to see how you overcome adversity.

Your unique response:

24. Why do you want to leave your present job?

Thought process:
This is an important question to an interviewer that will give them some good insight to who you are. The interviewer wants to see if you are running away from something or running toward an opportunity. They want to know if you are a "job hopper" or if you can be stable in a position. Are you leaving because of career advancement, or is there a conflict at your present company such as an inability to work with a supervisor? Make sure you respond positively no matter why you want to make a change. Focus on about experiences or skills you bring to the table and how they will benefit the new company.

Sample response:
I have had a good career with Bartz Seafood Company. I have won multiple awards for teamwork and productivity, and have been able to grow my career within this organization. Since this is a small company, I have come to the point where there isn't any more room for growth. I believe I have a lot more to offer, and I desire more of a challenge. From what I have researched about Ender Organic Foods, I am very intrigued with the challenges of this position and feel that this would be a great step that would utilize my skills and provide me room for growth.

POWERHOUSE POINTER: "A wise man will make more opportunities than he finds" (Sir Francis Bacon). Never speak negatively about a previous company or manager. Be able to explain company or career changes positively and always mention what skills and experiences you learned on the way.

Your unique response:

_____

_____

_____

_____

_____

_____

_____

25. How do you keep yourself organized?

Thought process:
The interviewer is looking for examples of your organizational skills. This could include organization of time management with day planner, calendar, or to-do list, or systematic organization such as a physical filing system or a system used on the computer. Provide an example and explain how it benefits you.

Sample response for both an experienced or new professional:
To be effective, it is very important that I make the most out of my day. I plan my day the night before. I put together a to-do list and cross-reference it with my appointments that I have for that day. I keep my schedule on my computer and also on my handheld so that I am never without my daily tasks as well my upcoming commitments. I find that by doing this, I don't forget to do something, I am well prepared, and I am able to utilize my time efficiently.

POWERHOUSE POINTER: "Plans are nothing; planning is everything" (Dwight D. Eisenhower). Organization and planning are keys to success. Showing a manager you take it upon yourself to be organized and plan your work shows commitment to professionalism.

Your unique response:

_____

_____

_____

_____

_____

_____

_____

26. What is one thing you would want to improve about yourself?

Thought process:
The interviewer wants to uncover any development areas you might have. He also wants to see if you can evaluate yourself in an objective way. There should always be something you want to improve on. It is not acceptable to say "nothing." Whatever you state, provide why you consider it an important improvement and what you have done proactively thus far.

Sample response for both an experienced and new professional: I would like to improve my communication skills. The ability to effectively communicate is vital to being successful. This is something I continue working on by asking for feedback from my peers and my manager.

 **POWERHOUSE POINTER:** If people didn't want to improve, there would never be any progress.

Your unique response:

27. What experience or skills have you gained that would be relevant to this position?

Thought process:
The interviewer wants to know what you are going to bring to the table. She is also going to use this information and compare it to other candidates. No matter your level of experience, provide examples that are relevant to this position. Your examples should include leadership, teamwork, work ethic, actual experience with the position, and so forth.

Sample response:
For this management position, my track record at ABC Metals demonstrates the success I have achieved in my professional career. I was able to learn from the ground up how to optimize factory production and increase output without increasing our fixed cost. In five years, I went from being on a team to managing my own production team. I believe the combination of these experiences will be beneficial to the position.

New professional response:
During college, I have had the opportunity to work individually and in groups. I am well adapted to being productive with either situation. I have a strong work ethic that translated to me being on the dean's list every semester. I have also found that I can be a leader when necessary, but I am also willing to learn and to be coached to make myself better.

POWERHOUSE POINTER: This is your time to shine and an opportunity to convince the interviewer that you are the perfect fit for this position. Make the most of it and don't hold back!

Your unique response:

28. If you were working with a group and there was not a designated leader, how would you take charge of the group?

Thought process:
The interviewer wants to gain more insight into how you work in a group environment. Are you a follower or a leader? If it were necessary, could you rise to the challenge and be a leader? How would you lead?

Sample response for both an experienced and new professional: I don't believe that you have to be the designated leader to lead. In a situation like this, I would immediately step up to take on some of the main responsibilities. I would start the communication process among the group to determine how we are going to accomplish our current objective. I would then work with the group to delegate the different tasks that needed to be accomplished. As a leader, I would make sure that everyone was involved and working together. The role of being a leader will then naturally take form. I have found from past experiences that making sure everyone is involved and contributing are the best ways to accomplish a common goal among a group. I think gaining trust and commitment is key to good leadership.

 **POWERHOUSE POINTER:** Tell me, I may listen. Teach me, I may remember. Involve me, I will do it.–Chinese Proverb

Your unique response:

29. What is your biggest weakness? Or where do you say you need the most improvement?

Thought process:
The interviewer is trying to gauge in which areas you feel you need help. He is trying to assess whether he would be able to help you in your development and growth. Also, the interviewer wants to see how you perceive yourself. *This answer will vary depending on your personality.*

Sample response:
An area of improvement I see for myself is my sense of urgency. By that I mean that I like to get the ball rolling and follow through until I am able to deliver an outcome. By working as a lead on a group project, I am learning to be more patient.

New professional response:
My biggest weakness is lack of experience. What I lack in experience though, I can make up with my drive and ability to quickly learn. Since I am fresh in the industry, I have no preconceived ideas or limitations. I am 100% committed to going above and beyond to be successful in the position.

POWERHOUSE POINTER: "No one is perfect and we will all make mistakes in business or our careers; the ones who learn from their mistakes and avoid repeating them will be successful" (J.L. Jones). No matter what your biggest weakness, being able to show that you have learned and grown from that experience is the most important issue.

Your unique response:

30. Have you ever been in a situation where you and your boss did not see eye to eye?

Thought process:
The interviewer is looking at your ability to be flexible. Are you open to seeing someone else's perspective? The interviewer is also looking for conflict resolution skills and your ability and willingness to work out a mutually beneficial outcome.

Sample response:
I remember recently when my manager and I were looking at notes from a recent team meeting and discussing how to proceed with a project. I had suggested we investigate and get more data before rolling out our new product. My boss thought that it would be best to go ahead and launch instead of delaying it by waiting for more data. I showed her the reasons for my concern. She listened and realized that there were some gaps in our information that did need to be filled. We decided on a hybrid model: commissioning a short study and then moving to launch. The outcome was a successfully launched product.

POWERHOUSE POINTER: When discussing conflicting points of view, it is best to focus the discussion on the issue and not the person involved.

Your unique response:

31. How does your experience (from another industry) qualify you for this position?

Thought process:
This is a great question for people who are switching careers. The interviewer wants to know what skills and experiences you bring that will make you successful in this new position. They also want to see if you have done your research on this new industry and if you have an understanding of the expectations of the job.

Sample response:
I have had a great career in the human resource department for five years, and I have gained valuable skills and experiences. Even though I have had good success, this is not what I have a passion to do. I quickly realized that I am a people person. During some routine field visits with our sales reps, I had the opportunity to see what they did on a day-to-day basis, and I immediately knew that I wanted to go into sales. In my prior positions, I have had the opportunity to develop my organization, presentation, and communication skills. I believe these skills coupled with my drive and desire to be successful will allow me to be a productive sales representative with your company.

POWERHOUSE POINTER: Do your homework before the interview and find parallels with your current career and your potential future career. Be able to show that you can take on these new challenges and be successful.

Your unique response:

32. How did your schooling prepare you for this job?

Thought process:
The interviewer wants to know more about your education and what you learned or skills you acquired. Many people go into careers that have nothing to do with their majors, so the interviewer wants to know how your education will translate into your success with this position. If you are interviewing for a position that deals directly with your major, then speak of your education in respect to that industry.

Sample response for both experienced and new professionals:
On top of a great education, college taught me a lot about organization, time management, people skills, and being self-driven and motivated. I know that these are essentials to be successful in this position, and I feel that these are some of my strongest qualities and skills. Throughout my college career, I was able to learn what worked and what didn't and ultimately how to make myself as productive as possible.

POWERHOUSE POINTER: You can always speak beyond the classroom when talking about your schooling. Include what you learned while being part of organizations, clubs, or other outside involvements you might have had.

Your unique response:

33. Why did you pick your major in college?

Thought process:
The interviewer wants to see if you had any calculated reasons as to why you chose your major. They want to understand what your interests were then and if they have changed? This also gives the interviewer an opportunity to learn more about your background and who you are. No matter what your major was, be sure to provide an explanation as to why you chose it. Do not say "I just picked something."

Sample response for both experienced and new professionals:
Since I was young, I always had an interest in building things. When I went to college I was interested in construction, but I was especially interested in the project management part of the job. I chose my major in project management my first semester because I knew that is what I wanted to do. I got a great education and even had the opportunity to do multiple internships that allowed me to gain some hands-on experience that I believe will help me accelerate my productivity in this position.

POWERHOUSE POINTER: It is always good to show a potential employer you create a plan of action for your major decisions and then how you implement that plan.

Your unique response:

34. How well do you work under deadlines?

Thought process:
The interviewer wants to learn about your organizational skills and how you handle the pressure of a deadline. Be sure to talk about organizing a strategy for the task at hand and how you will use your time and project management skills to accomplish meeting a deadline. Use examples from either your schooling or professional career.

Sample response:
I have had a lot of experience with deadlines in my current position as an electronic data specialist. Often I am given assignments that have to be finished in a specified time to meet contractual agreements between my company and the client. Once I find out the amount of time I am given for an assignment, I immediately break down the project to complete certain tasks each day. I always leave myself extra time in case I fall behind. Staying organized and using good time management skills have allowed me to complete all of my projects on time. My experience with this is something I think will be beneficial in this position, don't you agree?

New professional response:
College has given me some great experience dealing with deadlines. In most of my classes there were projects or assignments that had short deadlines or long deadlines that lasted the whole semester. I was able to learn to organize myself and use time management to handle both short and long duration projects. On top of that, I usually had to manage multiple deadlines at the same time. My experience with this is something I think will be beneficial to this position, don't you agree?

 **POWERHOUSE POINTER:** "The secret of all victory lies in the organization of the non-obvious." (Marcus Aurelius). Organization and time management of both major and minor details are important to success.

Your unique response:

_____

_____

_____

_____

_____

_____

_____

35. What type of salary are you looking for?

Thought process:
This is a tough question, and salary should never be brought up unless the interviewer mentions it first. This is also where pre-interviewing research comes in handy if you are able to find out what the average salary is in this particular position. You need to have some idea of what the position pays and what your value is. First ask the interviewer what the salary range is for the position, and then formulate your response. If you are new to the industry, you probably command the lower spectrum of the salary range than a more experienced professional. If you do ask for the higher spectrum of the salary range, be able to justify that with skills and experience that you will bring to the position.

Sample response for both experienced and new professionals: What is the salary range for this position? I am looking for a salary of *n*, but I am willing to be flexible given the economic environment and my interest in the position.

POWERHOUSE POINTER: It is always best to never bring up salary until the interviewer mentions it first. Be prepared for this question and try to decide on a realistic number. Always provide some flexibility and room for negotiating.

Your unique response:

36. What features you are looking for in a job?

Thought process:
The interviewer wants to see if you know what you are looking for in a job or career. People who know what they want tend to be more stable and will have more longevity in a position. They also want to see if your expectations are in line with the position they are offering. If it is not a good match, then there might be concerns about how you would fit into the position. Connect similarities between what you want to the job you are interviewing for.

Sample response for both experienced and new professionals:
It is important for me to be in a position where I am challenged to utilize my skills and to also develop and grow as a professional. I want to be with a company that provides the opportunity to advance my career. Through my research, I believe Olfers Investments offers the challenges and opportunities that I am looking for to have a long and successful career. I also like that there is a management training program in place, which tells me that the company wants to develop their professionals. This position is exactly what I am looking for.

POWERHOUSE POINTER: When you talk about wanting to take on challenges and grow your career, it tells the interviewer that you are willing to work hard and that you are looking for longevity with the company. Make sure these points are expressed in your response.

Your unique response:

37. What is the most recent skill you have learned in your career?

Thought process:
The interviewer will use this question to find out if you are managing the development of your skill set with your position. They also want to see what skills you have or might lack. Think of something that you have recently learned that has helped make you more productive or do your job more efficiently.

Sample response:
As an operations manager, I was recently given the responsibility of compiling weekly data for our unit and presenting it in a monthly meeting using Power Point. In the position I was in I had not had an opportunity to present to a group. I only had a basic working knowledge of Power Point and basic presentation skills. I spent time during the weekends to study and refine my presentation skills and learn the latest about Power Point. Now I can put together top quality presentations. The vice president of our company even made a comment to me about how professional my presentation looked.

POWERHOUSE POINTER: "The most important thing I've learned, is to keep learning" (J.L. Jones). It is impressive to show how you have taken the initiative to develop and advance your skill set. This shows employers that you are driven and self-motivated.

Your unique response:

_____

_____

_____

_____

_____

_____

_____

38. How have you improved as a manager? Or how do you keep improving as a manager?

Thought process:
The interviewer wants to gain a better understanding of how you have grown and evolved in a management role. They want to see if you are continuing to improve on your skills and capabilities, or if you just settle for the status quo. Provide examples of skills, management philosophies, or experiences you have gained that have made you a better manager.

Sample response:
To be a successful manager, I believe that I always have to be open to improving various aspects of myself. When I first became a manager, I was sometimes reluctant to delegate too much responsibility to my team. I was trying to learn about my team, their strengths and their weaknesses. Once I understood their different strengths and weaknesses, I was able to make sure everyone was contributing in a way that made them and the team successful. This has helped me manage top producing teams.

POWERHOUSE POINTER: "To improve is to change; to be perfect is to change often" (Winston Churchill). There is significance with any type of improvement as long as you try to put in the effort to be better.

Your unique response:

39. What is your management philosophy?

Thought process:
The interviewer wants to gain a deeper insight on how you manage people. They want to know what techniques or processes you use to make your team productive and successful. They are wanting to find answers to questions such as: are you hands on, do you micro-manage, are you good at delegating responsibility, how do you keep your team motivated, what are some of the traits you have learned that have made you a more effective manager?

Sample response:
I believe to be a successful and effective manager you have to have collaboration within your team. I work very hard to ensure everyone understands their role. I also take great pride in having everyone play a part in accomplishing the main goal. When the goal is accomplished, having the entire team share in the success reinforces the behaviors that are important to future success. I find that this motivates people to do their job well. My experience as a manager has also taught me to be adaptable and analyze situations quickly, but not to make quick decisions or jump to conclusions. It is important to determine an appropriate response by gaining additional information and then to take action. Since everyone is unique, I cater my management style to fit their personalities, which has lead to happy and productive employees. With my track record of leading successful teams, I am confident that these qualities will make me successful with your organization.

 **POWERHOUSE POINTER:** "The conventional definition of management is getting work done through people, but real management is developing people through work" (Agha Hasan Abedi).

Your unique response:

40. How do you motivate people as a manager?

Thought process:
The interviewer wants to know how you keep people motivated to do their jobs effectively and be productive. Use an example in your answer of a time when you successfully motivated your team to accomplish a goal, hit a quota, or meet a deadline.

Sample response:
I think it is very important to fully explain how a person's role contributes to accomplishing the main goal. This provides a sense of meaning to what they do. By accomplishing the main goal, it will make them successful and the team successful. Once a person understands this, they are usually self-motivated to do their best. I remember that we used to have a product that was at a very mature stage in its lifecycle. Keeping motivated was a challenge. When we got our new sales objectives, the sales people were very discouraged; they felt the goal was unrealistic. Once I broke down the goal into monthly incremental units, the team realized that the goal was not unrealistic. In fact they thought it was too easy. We not only met the goal that year but exceeded it by 10 percent!

 **POWERHOUSE POINTER:** "Leadership: The art of getting someone else to do something you want done because he wants to do it" (Dwight D. Eisenhower)

Your unique response:

41. What professional traits do you look for when hiring someone?

Thought process:
The interviewer wants to see if you know what to look for when hiring someone and what traits are important to you. They also want to see what type of experience you have with interviewing, and if you have been successful in hiring talented, productive people. It is good to use an example of someone you hired who has advanced their career within the organization.

Sample response:
I look for a combination of traits when hiring someone. Their background and experience provides a foundation and starting point, but I also try to find out more about the person. I want people who are responsible, driven, and want to develop and grow in their careers. Two years ago I hired a sales rep that had little experience in our industry. I was really impressed with his preparation for the interview and the energy he possessed. I took a chance on hiring him over someone who was more experienced. He became one of our top sales reps and has just recently accepted a promotion as a district sales manager in our Chicago branch.

POWERHOUSE POINTER: Managers who are poor at interviewing and make bad judgments on personnel decisions can cost a company greatly. The type of judgment you have about character speaks a lot about you as an individual.

Your unique response:

42. How do you handle terminating someone?

Thought process:
Letting someone go is a difficult part of being a manager, but it is part of the responsibilities of the position. The interviewer wants to gain insight on the type of person you are and how you would handle a delicate situation like this. Provide an example of a situation where you had to terminate someone. Be sure to explain why you had to do it and what actions you took in the process. If you never had to terminate someone, address the fact that you have been fortunate to have not been in that position, but if it was necessary, you would be able to handle that responsibility.

Sample response:
Recently my previous company went through a downsizing. Employees were randomly selected to be let go. One of my most tenured designers Catrina was selected in the downsizing. I let Catrina know that the downsizing had nothing to do with her performance and that unfortunately, due to the economic climate, the organization had to make cutbacks. Out of respect for her and the contributions she made to our organization, I asked her how she wanted me to share this information with the rest of the team. I assured her I would be a reference if she ever needed one and that I would keep my eyes and ears open for any opportunities that became available.

POWERHOUSE POINTER: Terminating an employee can be very stressful to a manager. Take time to think about how you are going to handle the situation before you speak to the person. Always maintain complete professionalism and confidentiality with delicate matters like this.

Your unique response:

43. How would your subordinates describe you?

Thought process:
This is another way for the interviewer to gain insight into your managerial approach. They are trying to assess how your management style will align with your future subordinates based on the views of those from your last company. They want to make sure you will be a good fit with the team that is already in place.

Sample response:
People on my team would say that I am fair, driven, and accountable. I am also approachable and willing to listen to suggestions or disagreements about any topic. I believe that having this open communication fosters an environment for people to share new ideas or solutions to problems. My subordinates know that I truly care about and will help them to accomplish their career goals. I pride myself on my ability to develop people. In fact, I have had three members of my team get promotions within our company in the past two years.

POWERHOUSE POINTER: "It's a lot easier for you to adapt to ten people, then trying to make ten people adapt to you. Sometimes when taking on a new management position, you might have to relearn how to be a manager" (J.L. Jones).

Your unique response:

_____

_____

_____

_____

_____

_____

_____

_____

Sales Interview Questions

44. What do you think is the most challenging aspect of being a sales representative?

Thought process:
This is an attempt for the interviewer to determine if you know the true challenges a sales representative faces on a daily basis. He is also trying to determine if you have the skills to meet these challenges. This is where your research on the position comes in handy. Use that knowledge to address the challenges of the position and how your skills will help you overcome them.

Sample response:

I think there are two challenges to being a sales representative. The first challenge is getting past the gatekeeper (these could be receptionists, secretaries or administrative assistants that are the point of contact for the customer you are targeting) and determining who the decision makers (these are the people who will actually make the decision to buy a product or service) are. You have to be creative in finding a way to gain access to them. The second challenge is to truly understanding the dynamics of the territory, which include the customers and the competition.

 **POWERHOUSE POINTER:** Challenges are part of any job. How you overcome those challenges is what is most important. If you are currently in sales and face these obstacles in your present job, be sure to include examples of how you deal with these in your answer.

Your unique response:

45. Do you like to win or hate to lose?

Thought process:
The interviewer is looking to see what truly motivates you. The joy experienced in winning or the fear of losing. It does not matter which one motivates you as long as you can explain why. Remember a situation where you won a deal and tell the manger what motivated you. Or you can use a team example.

Sample response:
I hate to lose. We had a sales contest in our region to see who could sell the most communication systems in a quarter. The prize was $1000. I ended up coming in second, and it bothered me. It would have been nice to win the money, but even better to win the contest. This just motivates me more to push myself that much harder next time.

New professional response:
In high school I was on a football team that had built a great tradition of winning year after year. Our coach instilled in us a motto of "We love to win, but we hate to lose even more." I still hold that belief today, and it's what pushes me to always try to be successful. I feel that because of this, I learned a lot about self-discipline and self-motivation.

POWERHOUSE POINTER: "People often say that motivation doesn't last. Well, neither does bathing - that's why we recommend it daily." (Zig Ziglar)

Your unique response:

46. Why should we hire you? You do not have any sales experience.

Thought process:
The interviewer is trying to determine what qualities you possess that would make you successful in sales. She wants to see how driven and persuasive you are. Do not focus on your lack of experience, acknowledge it and then disarm it. You must build a logical argument for her so she sees you as a natural fit for the position.

Sample response:
Although I have not held a direct sales position, I have had to sell ideas and concepts within my company. For example, there was a time when I had to sell a budget increase to complete a project. I had to pitch the idea to upper management. I met with resistance in the beginning, but I explained the importance of the project to the overall success of our organization. I also made sure I spoke with all who were involved in the decision-making process. With continued persistence, I was able to convince them to approve the budget increase. I feel that I have the drive, energy, and communication skills needed to be effective in sales.

New professional response:
I have always had great communication skills, and I feel I am good at working with people. I understand the basics of the sales process and the organization and discipline that's required to be successful. I proved this by putting myself through school and maintaining great grades. Even though I might lack some experience, I will overcome that by outworking my competition. I have been raised with a strong work ethic and I am very money motivated. If given the opportunity, I know I will be a contributing member to your team.

 **POWERHOUSE POINTER:** "Experience is simply the name we give our mistakes" (Oscar Wilde). Experience is great to have, but not a necessity when interviewing.

Your unique response:

_____

_____

_____

_____

_____

_____

_____

47. Sell me this product (e.g., this pen).

Thought process:
This is the age-old topic that is brought up in most sales interviews, especially if the interviewee has no previous sales experience. The interviewer is looking to see if you know the sales process. Do you understand how to build rapport? Do you probe and determine why the product could provide a solution? What are the client's needs? Is the product even the best choice? Primarily though, the interviewer wants to see how you think on your feet. He also wants to see if you *ask for the business*.

Sample response for both an experienced and new professional:

Think of the five steps of a sale:

1. *Qualify the decision maker.* Are you the person in charge of purchasing pens at XYZ Company?

2. *Determine your competition.* What kinds of pen are you currently using at XYZ Company?

3. *Investigate likes and dislikes.* What do you like about the pen that you're currently using? What don't you like about the pen you're currently using?

4. *Offer features and benefits.* Our pen has all of the qualities that you like in the pen that you're currently using but with a longer-lasting ink well.

5. *Close.* If you order five boxes now, I can offer you 20 percent off.

 **POWERHOUSE POINTER:** Make sure you ask the buyer questions. You cannot sell something to people if you do not know what they want to buy. This is a question where you can really distinguish yourself with your creativity.

Your unique response:

48. Tell me about the sales process. What is the most important phase of a sales process?

Thought process:
The interviewer is looking for your understanding of the entire sales process. This list is very basic, but provides a good foundation to develop a response:

- Opening the call
- Understanding the situation
- Probing for problems
- Exploring implications
- Probing for needs
- Matching product attributes to needs
- Overcoming objections
- Closing

Sample response for both an experienced and new professional: The sales process first involves identifying the decision maker. Once that has been established, properly opening the call, understanding the situation, probing for problems, exploring implications of the problems, gaining agreement on needs, demonstrating how the product meets those needs, and closing for the business all have to be addressed.

POWERHOUSE POINTER: You can try to close a sale all you want, but if you don't know the needs of the customer or effectively demonstrate your product meeting those needs, then you are wasting your time and the customer's time.

Your unique response:

49. How would you go about persuading someone to see your point of view? Give examples.

Thought process:
The interviewer is looking to see how persuasive you are and how well you can communicate a thought or idea. She wants to see how you can take a concept and have it resonate with the customer. Use a personal example in this response of a time you successfully persuaded someone.

Sample response for both an experienced and new professional:
I would first disarm any barriers between my point of view and the other person's point of view. I would do this by validating the other person's opinion and then discussing the benefits of my opinion. Keeping their opinion in mind, I would then draw parallels to my point of view and the solution of the problem. (Use a personal or professional situation as an example)

POWERHOUSE POINTER: Remember that you do not have to persuade people the first time you meet them. Selling is a process.

Your unique response:

50. What makes a good salesperson? What qualities do you possess that make you a good salesperson?

Thought process:
The interviewer wants to know what you think are the characteristics of a good salesperson and which of those qualities you will bring to the position. If he understands what you believe are important attributes of a salesperson, then he will understand more about your personality. This also provides him with the ability to see your strengths as a salesperson.

Sample response for both an experienced and new professional: I believe a quality salesperson has to be persistent, driven, amiable, organized, and flexible. No matter what adversity might come up, you have to be persistent and flexible. You also have to be organized to manage a territory or an account effectively. Of course, a good salesperson should be amiable and able to build and grow relationships for the future. These are qualities that I bring to the table that will help me be successful.

 **POWERHOUSE POINTER:** Great sales people = strong work ethic and discipline

Your unique response:

51. Does money motivate you?

Thought process:
Don't be afraid to say that you are money-motivated; most sales people are. You do not want to come across as a money-hungry person, but you do want to let the hiring manager know that money does motivate you.

Sample response for both an experienced and new professional:
I think you need to balance the importance of a career with obtainable financial rewards. If I were not money-motivated, I would not be in sales.

POWERHOUSE POINTER: Sales people are some of the highest-paid professionals around the world.

Your unique response:

52. What do you consider your greatest sales accomplishment and why?

Thought process:
The interviewer is trying to understand what is professionally important to you. You can talk about an account you won or a sales award that you received. Speak to the accomplishment and how you achieved it.

Sample response:
I had a target customer that I tried to call on for a long time, but he would never see me. I stayed persistent in trying to see him. On my fourth visit to this client, anticipating that I would be turned away, I was pleasantly surprised when he took me back to his office and spoke to me about my product. He mentioned that he had a falling out with my competitor, and he was looking for a new supplier. I also learned that he had read the information that I had been leaving behind and had visited our Website. I didn't get a sale that day, but he did buy from me after a couple of follow-up visits. This taught me to never give up. You never know when the circumstances might change to your favor.

POWERHOUSE POINTER: Persistence and accomplishment go hand in hand.

Your unique response:

53. What if you are working a solid forty-hour workweek and sales were still flat in your territory?

Thought process:
The interviewer is looking for your work ethic, a sense of urgency, and the ability to be creative in identifying new strategies to increase sales. Working smarter can be more productive than working harder. Don't just say that you will put in extra hours, provide a plan of action.

Sample response:
I encountered this situation once before. Knowing that some of my top customers ate breakfast at 5:30 a.m. at the local diner, I decided to get up early to join them for breakfast. None of my competitors were doing this, so I felt that it might give me an advantage. I was able to further develop my relationships with these customers, which led to a better understanding of the issues they faced. With this information I was able to provide more suitable product solutions, which led to an increase in my sales.

 **POWERHOUSE POINTER:** When discussing sales downturns, do not make excuses: provide solutions.

Your unique response:

54. How do you distinguish yourself when you are selling a commodity product?

Thought process:
The interviewer is evaluating your selling skills. She is also trying to see how you would differentiate your product from the competition. This is an opportunity to show your creative side and also speak to examples of what makes you different from other sales reps.

Sample response:
If I am in a market where the products and pricing are the same, I make sure I know and understand my customers better than the competition. I find out if there are issues that my customers are facing. If so, I try to find a way that I can go the extra mile to help them. I feel confident that having stronger and deeper relationships with my customers helps me gain the sale.

POWERHOUSE POINTER: Share an example of when you went above and beyond the call of duty and got the business. This will help distinguish you from other candidates.

Your unique response:

55. How did you turn a "hostile" relationship into a sale?

Thought process:
The interviewer is assessing your conflict-resolution skills. He wants to see your tenacity and your ability to find common ground with a customer. The interviewer is looking for a situation you were placed in, the action you took, and what resulted as a consequence.

Sample response:
First, I always address these issues with my manager or supervisor to discuss appropriate ways to handle these situations according to company policy. I inherited an account in which the client had been using our equipment for the last ten years and had just dropped us. The client had experienced below-standard customer service from the previous sales representative. As a result this client said he would never buy another piece of equipment from us again. I did not take it personally but listened and let the client know I understood his frustration. I explained that I didn't expect anything, but just wanted to be given the opportunity to prove myself and nothing more. I was able to regain the client's trust by being patient and persistent. Over the next several months, I was able to grow and nurture a relationship with this client that eventually allowed me to gain back his business.

POWERHOUSE POINTER: Don't let a customer's hostile attitude affect you personally. Remember to think about the situation, your actions, and the resulting outcome.

Your unique response:

56. In the past what have you done to increase sales for an already established territory?

Thought process:
The interviewer is looking for your ability to analyze your territory and identify areas where there is additional business potential. They are looking for the specific steps you took that made you successful. Also, the interviewer is looking for the attitude that there are always more sales to be made, even in accounts that look tapped out.

Sample response:
I inherited a territory that had revenues of $1.5 million annually. At first glance the territory market share looked tapped out, and I knew I would have a challenge to increase revenues. Instead of thinking of ways to get my customers to buy more from me, I helped them with their efforts in promoting to their customers. This increased their sales which in-turn increased mine. By thinking outside the box and identifying new ways to drive up demand, I was able to increase sales to $2.5 million. That was 40 percent above quota.

POWERHOUSE POINTER: Tapped out is relative: there is always gold to be mined. Be specific to show how the success is directly attributable to your efforts.

Your unique response:

57. Tell me about your current customers and current products. Give examples.

Thought process:
The interviewer is looking to see what type of relationships you have built with your customers. She wants to know how and why you are able to increase sales. She is looking to see how you leverage long-term business relationships and increase market penetration within each account. The interviewer also wants to see how you talk about your customers and current products.

Sample response:
I currently call on ten large accounts and am responsible for increasing business in each of these accounts by 20 percent this year. They are current customers who are using our products. Fortunately I have great relationships with these accounts. In fact, I am usually first to know if there are any problems or changes with their current purchasing structure. I found out at the beginning of the year that they were going to have to make a change in all of types of paper goods they purchased to meet a code of only using items that were partially recycled. By understanding their situation and probing for additional needs, I was able to match them with a product we carried and increase my product sales by 35 percent in each account!

 **POWERHOUSE POINTER:** Never talk disparagingly about your customers or products. If you don't have something good to say, don't say anything at all.

Your unique response:

58. What is your perception of a typical day as a sales representative?

Thought process:
The interviewer is looking for your perception of what a sales representative does on a daily basis. He is also looking for work ethic and commitment to getting the job done. The more you can draw parallels between your experiences and the sales position you are interviewing for, the more effective you will be.

Sample response for both an experienced and new professional: As a representative I would phone and meet as many leads as possible. I would stay organized and maintain my current client base. I would make sure to analyze my data and update information I gathered throughout the day. At the end of the day, I believe it is important to look over pre-call planning for my next day to make sure I am prepared and being as productive as possible. If the company policy permits, I would also entertain my clients to further develop my relationships.

POWERHOUSE POINTER: If you do not have sales experience, make sure you demonstrate your willingness and ambition to learn this position.

Your unique response:

59. If you were to get this position, how would you approach your territory?

Thought process:
The interviewer is looking for someone who can plan and organize. She wants to see how you go about planning your actions and meeting a specific set of goals. This would be a good time to present your Powerhouse 30–60–90 Day Action Plan.

Sample response for both an experienced and new professional: I would first review the history of the territory. Then I would analyze the information and look for trends. Depending on what I saw, I would formulate a plan that could be measured by both short-term and long-term goals. I would make sure these goals were in line with my manager's expectations, and then I would put that plan to action. After the first 30, 60, and 90 days, I would re-evaluate my progress, and alter my plan accordingly.

POWERHOUSE POINTER: "He who fails to plan, plans to fail" (Proverb quote). Plan your work and work your plan.

Your unique response:

60. Give me an example of how you can get to the decision makers when others can't.

Thought process:
The interviewer is trying to see if you have the ability to overcome obstacles. He also wants to see if you are a self-initiator or need direction to continue in the face of adversity. Incorporate an example from your own experience and discuss how you addressed the challenge.

Sample response:
I pride myself on being able to develop unique solutions for my customers. There was a large account in the Midwest that had a relationship with our competitor for over a decade. They were not even willing to let me come in and speak to them about our product line. After a year of trying to get their business, I tried something that no one from our company had done before. The next time I called their office, instead of trying to set up an appointment with the purchasing manager, I asked if it would be possible for me to talk to one of their sales reps. I set up a day to spend time in the field with one of their sales reps. I learned more about the company in that one day than I had from a decade's worth of notes. Because of this, I changed my approach and was finally able to get in front of a key decision maker.

POWERHOUSE POINTER: "Energy and persistence conquer all things" (Benjamin Franklin).

Your unique response:

61. How do you plan your business call activities?

Thought process:
The interviewer is looking to see how you organize your schedule for appointments and plan your day. Make sure to provide personal examples that highlight your organizational and time management skills.

Sample response:
I make plans every Sunday evening for the following week based on scheduled appointments. This involves pre-call planning for each account and setting the goal for each sales call. For customers I do not have appointments with, I determine what the best days and times to meet with them are and then try to schedule accordingly. I make sure I provide flexibility in my schedule to deal with cancellations or last-minute scheduled appointments. At the end of every day, I keep a customer log to track my progress and provide notes that will help me on the next sales call.

POWERHOUSE POINTER: Make sure to take good sales call notes; they help you prepare for your next sale calls.

Your unique response:

_____

_____

_____

_____

_____

_____

_____

62. How do you prioritize accounts within your territory?

Thought process:
The interviewer wants to determine that you set your priorities so that you get the best return on your time investment. You should organize your territory based on calling the customers with the greatest sales potential. He is looking to see if you know the "80/20 rule" that states, 80 percent of your business comes from 20 percent of your customers.

Sample response:
I would analyze my territory and determine the accounts that have the greatest sales potential. I would work to determine the top 20 percent of my clients and start pursuing their business. Once I felt comfortable with my relationships and sales growth, I would then explore the rest of my customers and develop new clients.

POWERHOUSE POINTER: Working smarter is more effective than just working hard.

Your unique response:

_____

_____

_____

_____

_____

_____

_____

63. How do you gain access to a decision maker?

Thought process:
The interviewer is looking for your thought process, creativity, and tenacity. She wants to see if you can identify the decision makers within an organization and how you go about the process. Provide examples of how you connected with the gatekeepers that led you to the decision maker.

Sample response:
In a previous account that I used to call on, I researched the company and made contacts within the organization starting with the receptionist. I developed relationships with these contacts who eventually directed me to the person I needed to talk to regarding my product line. Through these contacts I was able to get an appointment with the key decision maker, which resulted in a successful sale.

POWERHOUSE POINTER: Never underestimate the importance of any person within an organization; you never know whom they might be connected with.

Your unique response:

64. How would you build a virgin territory? Tell me your thought process.

Thought process:
The interviewer is looking for your thought process and business logic. He wants to see how you would take ownership and the creativity with which you would approach the business. He does not want to know just the "what" but also the "how."

Sample response for both an experienced and new professional: First, I would study the dynamics and market potential of the territory. I would then try to understand the competition in my geography and how they affect my accounts. I would then analyze my customers based on size and potential. Once I determined my short-term and long-term goals, I would develop a strategic plan of action for each account. I would review this plan with my manager to make sure she agreed with my approach and make any adjustments if needed. Monthly, I would evaluate my sales results and adjust my action plan to ensure that I met my objectives.

POWERHOUSE POINTER: Spend quality time putting together a plan of action; it will be your road map to success and save you time and frustration later on.

Your unique response:

65. Give an example of when you failed in sales. How did you handle rejection, conflict? Give specifics.

Thought process:
The interviewer wants to see how you deal with adversity. No matter what example you give, show that you have learned from the situation and you are able to use that experience to further your career today.

Sample response:
I worked on an account that did yearly contracts with their suppliers. Even though I clearly showed my product was superior and I could help with overall costs, the manager decided to go with my competitor. I was somewhat discouraged because of all the hard work and effort I had put into this account. I came to find out that the manager was good friends with my competitor. I continued to maintain my professional relationship with the company. Before the next contract negotiations came up, that manager left the company. Because I had maintained a good professional relationship with the company, they rewarded me with the following year's contract. I learned that you need to always stay professional and maintain your relationships because you never know when the door to an opportunity might open.

POWERHOUSE POINTER: "A failure is a man who has blundered but is not capable of cashing in on the experience." (Elbert Hubbard) We have all made mistakes or have had failures in our life; remember to show the interviewer how you have grown and learned from those experiences.

Your unique response:

66. Give an example of an obstacle that you had to overcome in sales.

Thought process:
Once again, the interviewer wants to see how you take on challenges. The interviewer wants to see that you properly identified an issue and developed a plan of action to overcome the challenge. Make sure that when you describe this issue, you talk about the situation, the action you took toward solving the problem, the outcome, and what you learned from the experience.

Sample response:
When I was working for a fertilizer company, our product was perceived to be more expensive than the competition because the size of the bags were not the industry standard. I worked with our marketing department to formulate a plan that would alert our customers to the size difference. Once our customers realized they were paying the same amount based on volume, the problem was eliminated.

POWERHOUSE POINTER: "The greater the obstacle, the more glory in overcoming it" (Molière). There will always be challenges in business; successful people are not afraid to take those challenges head on.

Your unique response:

- Returning to school
  - exception
  - family balance
- [illegible]
  - Created [illegible] DB
    - Maintain data for [illegible]
    - part of deliv.
    - 20% [illegible]

67. What makes you special in sales, and how do you differentiate yourself from your peers?

Thought process:
This is an opportunity to talk about what separates you from other job candidates. Reiterate your qualities and then talk about what special traits you bring to the table. If it comes down to a close decision between you and another candidate, the interviewer is going to have to weigh every issue. Make sure you talk about going the extra mile and doing whatever is appropriate to be successful.

Sample response:
I have a strong work ethic, I am very organized, and I pride myself in the knowledge of my product and competition. I believe my people skills and my ability to build long-lasting relationships is what makes me special in sales. I make it a point to spend a little bit of extra time to really get to know my customers. This usually helps me to better understand what their needs are and tailor my sales approach accordingly. No matter who my competitor is or what they do, I will do that much more to be better. This drive is what I believe separates me from my peers.

POWERHOUSE POINTER: "Good things come to those who wait, but great things come to those who hustle" (Abraham Lincoln).

Your unique response:

68. What do you do when a prospect is sitting on a contract or stalling and will not sign the deal?

Thought process:
The potential employer wants to see how you evaluate problems. They also would like to gain insight about how deliberate and thorough you are in trying to understand the underlying issues. They also want to see how you devise solutions and how persistent you are in trying to gain a commitment.

Sample response:
First, I want to identify why there is a delay in finalizing the sale. There may be multiple reasons. Some of the reasons may include need for additional information, a competing offer, or budget constraints. I would follow up with the decision maker to make sure that we were on the same page about what the issues are. I would then work closely with the decision maker to try and develop a solution that would benefit both parties.

 **POWERHOUSE POINTER:** "Drive thy Business or it will drive thee" (Benjamin Franklin).

Your unique response:

69. How do you generate and create your leads?

Thought process:
The potential employer is looking for an individual's creativity and drive. They also want to see the entrepreneurial spirit of an individual and how that person "thinks out of the box"?

Sample response:
I use a variety of sources: I make cold calls by using the good old traditional yellow page method, major lead sources such as a Hoovers database, networking events, alliances, partnerships, and one of the best is customer referrals as they come with money to spend. I always update my existing customer base because it is much easier to sell to an existing customer than to sell to a new customer.

POWERHOUSE POINTER: Networking can present itself in many situations, take advantage of them all.

Your unique response:

Questions to Ask the Interviewer

Every interview provides the interviewee with the opportunity to ask questions. This is an excellent opportunity to ensure that you and your future employer share the same core values and that this is the right position for you. This part of the interviewing process is just as important as when you were answering questions. Asking the right questions can have a greater positive impact than others. Knowing which ones are positively received will enable you to leave the interviewer with a good impression. The ability to ask good questions will show your thought process and the time you put into researching the position. It will also allow the interviewer to address any concerns or issues you might have. During this part of the interview, you will have the opportunity to learn more details about the position than might have been previously discussed.

We have provided sample questions that cover five categories: the company, the job opportunity, the interviewer, summary, and closing. Read the sample questions for each topic and make notes of how to personalize each question for your interview.

Remember, this workbook is only as effective as the effort you put into it. Do your research on the potential company and ask questions that are of interest or concern to you.

 **POWERHOUSE POINTER:** Make sure to do research on the company you are interviewing with so you can formulate intelligent questions. Asking questions that could have been answered on a company Website will show lack of preparation.

The Company

- With the ever-changing dynamics in the market, how does Company XYZ plan to grow and compete?
- How would a leadership change at the top impact the current momentum?
- How does Company XYZ foster creativity and innovation?
- What challenges does the company face against the competition?
- How does an economic slowdown affect the company?

The Job Opportunity

- What was the background of the last two or three people who had this position?
- Where are they today?
- What will be expected of me in the first two to six months?

- What are some examples of superior performance in the position?
- Why is this position open?
- Where can this position lead in regards to future advancement?

The Interviewer

- How did you get to where you are today?
- How do you describe your management philosophy/style?
- What do you like best about working for this company?
- Where do you see yourself in the next five years?
- What is the toughest challenge you face?
- What do you look for in a good employee?

POWERHOUSE POINTER: Remember, people like to talk about themselves. Make these questions engaging.

Summary (If there are multiple interviewers, ask each interviewer.)

- If you could change one thing about this company, what would that be?
- What situation will I know about six months from now that I'll wish I had known about today?

Closing

- Do you see me as a good fit for the position?
- Is there anything I shared with you that needs further clarification?
- How do my qualifications compare with others you have hired?
- Is there any reason that we can't arrange the next step for the interview process here and now?
- I want to be considered for this position. I am very interested in working for you.

Powerhouse Tips for a Successful Interview

1. Arrive ten to fifteen minutes early.

2. Bring two clean copies of your résumé to any interview. If you are going to be interviewed by more than two people, then bring enough copies for everyone there.

3. Most interviews last one hour. Allow yourself ample time. Do not try and schedule too many things around the time of your interview.

4. The way you dress makes a statement about you. Dressing in a professional manner will make a favorable impression. Most interviewers appreciate and look for a well-dressed professional.

5. Once you arrive at the location for the interview, treat anyone you encounter with professionalism and a positive attitude. You never know who you might meet and what influence they might have on the hiring decision, so you want to make sure you give off a great impression to everyone.

6. Always maintain a professional image in the interview. Even if the interviewer has a casual approach, make sure to keep up your professionalism and use appropriate manners. You never know when you are being tested!

7. Give a firm handshake and look the interviewer in the eye.

8. Sometimes your nonverbal behaviors say more than your verbal. Keep you posture, smile, maintain eye contact throughout the interview, and slightly lean forward (as this shows attentiveness and interest). Don't slouch or fidget, and pay attention to your facial expressions and use occasional head nods to reinforce what is being said.

9. When you are asked a question, it is good to repeat the question to clarify and then pause to collect your thoughts and formulate a response.

10. If you can't get to the interview on time, call the interviewer to notify them immediately.

11. Don't discuss salary or benefits; let the interviewer bring this up first.

12. Always ask for business cards or contact information from those who interviewed you.

13. Close the interview with a firm handshake and by asking for the position.

14. If this is the first interview and the interviewer has indicated that the process involves multiple interviews, ask what the next steps are in the hiring process. Ask to be included in the process.

15. Before you leave the interview, make sure you understand the hiring process. If this is the first interview and the interviewer has indicated that the process involves multiple interviews, ask what the next steps are in the hiring process. Ask to be included in the process.

POWERHOUSE POINTER: When answering a question during an interview, remember to stay focused and to the point. Be thorough with your response, but don't oversell or veer off the subject.

The Brag Book

A brag book is used to show successes and accomplishments you have achieved throughout your schooling and/or career. It is a powerful visual tool that makes you memorable to the interviewer. The brag book should include awards, rankings, e-mails, yearly reviews, and any other type of acknowledgments that highlight your success. When putting your brag book together, keep it in chronological order and in a way that is easy to present to an interviewer. If you have received trophies or plaques, take pictures of them to include in your brag book. Be ready to speak in detail about what you have included and explain why it is significant. Always keep your brag book updated throughout your career. Check and modify your brag book before every interview for relevance to the opportunity you are pursuing. The brag book should ultimately provide additional information to the interviewer that distinguishes you from the other candidates.

If you are a recent college graduate or just starting your career for the first time, you might not have access to many accolades. Try to include anything you received during your schooling, recognition from a part-time job, organizations you belonged to, church/social groups, etc. The point is to highlight the successes to the various organizations/positions you have been involved with. These highlights can then be used to quantify the value you can bring to a certain position.

Don't worry about including too much information. As long is it is something that you can speak to that portrays you in a positive light, the more the better. Just like the name says, it's a "brag book." Don't be shy about you accomplishments. This is the time where it is okay to brag about yourself. In fact, if presented properly, the brag book could be the determining factor that an interviewer bases their final decision on between two candidates.

Powerhouse tips for the brag book:

- Make the brag book look neat and organized. Use folders or presentation binders to house the information.
- Keep the information in the brag book separated and in chronological order. Example: high school, college, and different positions you held.
- If you have awards, plaques, or trophies you have won, take pictures of them and write a brief description.
- Make sure you match up your highlights with the qualities of the position you are interviewing for.
- Keep your brag book updated throughout your career. It will save you time in the future, because you never know when you might need it.

 **POWERHOUSE POINTER:** It is good idea to include recommendation letters in your brag book. Keep your list of contacts for recommendation current throughout your career. Always give your recommendations a heads-up when you are interviewing so that they are not surprised if or when they are contacted by a prospective employer.

Plan Your Work, and Work Your Plan: Powerhouse 30–60–90 Day Action Plan

The Powerhouse 30–60–90 Day Action Plan is a proactive way to demonstrate to the interviewer your organizational skills and your plans to make this opportunity successful. It is set up as a presentation type of format so you can easily communicate what your action plan is for the position should you get hired. When putting together your Powerhouse 30–60–90 Day Action Plan, here are some things to consider:

- In the first thirty days, think about how you are going to learn and adjust to the position and the organization.

- Next, the sixty-day section should speak to how you are still learning, refining your skills, and soliciting feedback.

- Lastly, in the ninety-day section talk about how you are incorporating feedback and how you plan to follow up with team members, managers, and customers.

This action plan can also open up dialogue that could lead to more insight about the opportunity.

The Powerhouse 30–60–90 Day Action Plan could be presented at any point of the interview, it will depend when there is an appropriate opportunity. If the interviewer asks you a question about how you would take on the position or what your expectations are for the position, then it would be a proper time to introduce your Powerhouse 30–60–90 Day Action Plan. If an opportunity does not present itself during the interview, then the Powerhouse 30–60–90 Day Action Plan can be a great close to the interview. Since hiring is based traditionally on past experience, the Powerhouse 30–60–90 Day Action Plan is the chance for you to demonstrate to a potential employer what you are going to be able to do for them tomorrow.

We have put together two mock Powerhouse 30–60–90 Day Action Plans. The first example is non-specific for any type of position and the second is for sales position. Following the examples, space is provided for you to formulate your own plan. Make this plan specific to the position you are interviewing for. Include information and details about the position and company. Remember, you want to explain how you will take on the challenges in this role and contribute to the future success of the organization.

 **POWERHOUSE POINTER:** If you love what you do, it's really not work!

Powerhouse 30–60–90 Day Action Plan – General

_____

(Company Name)
30-Day Plan

- Quickly learn and familiarize myself with administrative processes and procedures.
- Get myself organized to be as efficient as possible in the position.
- Gain an understanding of the company culture.
- Meet with my manager to make sure expectations are fully understood.
- Attend team meetings and conference calls.
- Ask my manager or direct supervisor to recommend a mentor.
- Spend time with a mentor to gain additional insight to the position and company.
- If applicable, learn proprietary software and communication platform and process.
- Understand how my role interacts with other parts of the company.
- Meet my co-workers and individuals from other departments.
- Use all resources to learn who the internal and external gatekeepers are. Learn who the contacts are and how to access key people. Learn as much information about them as I can so I can accelerate relationships.

(Company Name)
60-Day Plan

- Continue organizing myself to optimize productivity.
- Follow up with my manager to see how I am progressing in my position.
- Incorporate my manager's feedback and identify areas for improvement and put together a development plan.
- Evaluate challenges in the position and ways to overcome them.
- Reinforce what I have learned from my mentor.
- Keep building relationships with co-workers and others within the company.
- Start to identify ways to contribute more.
- Set short-term and long-term goals for myself and markers against which to measure.
- Continue to educate myself to become a resource within the position.
- Polish personal skills and keep learning.

**(Company Name)
90-Day Plan**

- Continue to earn and build trust and respect from coworkers, customers, and clients.
- Solicit feedback from my manager and make sure I am progressing with my personal development plan.
- Gain a broader understanding of the company.
- Continue to grow and build rapport with customers and clients (if applicable).
- Take a personal recap to reevaluate goals and accomplishments. How am I doing? What have I done well? What can I improve on?
- Start documenting recognition and how I am making an impact.
- Start networking with other people in my profession to stay abreast of changes and new topics.
- Keep brainstorming ideas to continue to make myself as efficient and productive as possible.
- Continue toward success and *have fun!*

Powerhouse 30–60–90 Day Action Plan – Sales

(Company Name)
30-Day Plan

- Quickly learn and familiarize myself with administrative processes and procedures.
- Meet with my manager to make sure expectations are fully understood.
- Attend team meetings and conference calls.
- Learn all protocols for budget and acceptable actions that can be taken with customers and clients.
- Spend time with new product information to become an expert on (product).
- Learn and fully understand my competition (i.e., positives and negatives of competition) and how to compete and sell against them.
- Evaluate challenges in the territory and ways to overcome them.
- Understand how and why customers buy my product.
- Review marketing materials and pricing information for putting together a business action plan.
- Use all resources to learn who the internal and external gatekeepers are. Learn who the contacts are and how to access

key people. Learn as much information about them as I can so I can accelerate relationships.

- Start meeting as many customers as possible to build rapport.

(Company Name)
60-Day Plan

- Continue organization and refining of territory and continue to meet customers and clients to build relationships.
- Review and adjust schedule to make myself more efficient and effective in my position.
- Continue to probe and look for new opportunities.
- Analyze and understand why clients or customers are positioned where they are with my products and my competition.
- Keep probing for access to key customers.
- Keep up with changes in the market and with competition.
- Begin to brainstorm ideas to give myself a competitive edge in the market.
- Polish personal skills and keep learning.

(Company Name)
90-Day Plan

- Earn and build trust and respect from coworkers, customers, and clients.
- Find out what motivates individual customers to purchase our product. Continue learning about the perceptions of my service among my customers.
- Identify peer leaders in the industry and within the organization.
- Continue to grow business and develop new areas.
- Have a clear handle of goals, account potential, and direction.
- Solicit feedback from managers. What needs to be improved? What seems to be working well?
- Continue to grow and build rapport with customers and clients.
- Take a personal recap to reevaluate goals and accomplishments. How am I doing? What have I done well? What can I improve on?
- Continue toward success and *have fun!*

Your Unique 30–60–90 Day Business Plan

30-Day Plan

60-Day Plan

90-Day Plan

Post-interviewing Information

The post-interview is just as critical as the pre-interview planning and the interview itself. There are simple things that you can do that will help differentiate you from other candidates. This is also an opportunity for you to learn the areas you may need to improve your interviewing skills. Below is a list of Powerhouse tips that you can incorporate after your interview.

Powerhouse Tips for After the Interview

- Write down notes of critical information you picked up during the interview. This can be valuable information to use as you continue on to the next step of the interviewing process.

- Make notes of what you thought your strengths and weaknesses were in the interview. (Example: If you have an opportunity, ask the interviewer what areas that they think you can improve on.) Use this information to fine-tune your interview skills for your next interview.

- Immediately send a thank you letter to the interviewer(s); this can be easily done through a letter or an e-mail. A thank you letter allows you another opportunity to reiterate your interest and qualifications for the position.
- If you are using a recruiter, make sure to contact them immediately afterward to discuss the interview. Often times they will also have feedback for you. Take notes and any critiquing information as this will be beneficial should you have to interview again for other opportunities.
- If the employer says they will make a decision in a week, don't contact them before that. Wait until the said amount of time has passed before you follow up. When you do contact them, make sure to thank them again for the opportunity to interview and express your interest in the position.
- No matter what their decision is, always maintain a positive attitude. If they decide to go in a different direction, it's okay. Let them know if another opportunity becomes available that you would be interested. You never know when something might change or the person they hired didn't work out. Never burn a bridge. Not being offered a position does not always reflect something that has to do with you. Sometimes situations with open positions in a company change because of budget cuts, downsizing, internal hiring, etc. Just remember to use every interviewing opportunity as a chance to practice and learn. If you can take away something from the interview to make you better for future opportunities, then you come out a winner.

POWERHOUSE POINTER: Not being selected to participate in the next steps of the interview or being offered the job is just part of the interviewing process. Just remember to use every interviewing opportunity as a chance to practice and learn. It is important that you always handle it in a dignified way. Being a class act today will lead you to a bright future tomorrow.

Thank You Letters

Thank you letters are a critical component of the interviewing process. Think of the thank you letter as the closing chapter of your interview. The thank you letter is the last impression you make on a potential employer. Remember, your contacts have already met you in person. This letter should recap your strengths and reiterate what you will be able to provide the company. Include one main point from the interview to remind the interviewer who you are and what you can bring to the table. This is also another opportunity for you to ask for the position. Be sure to thank all interviewers for their time. Once again, this is an opportunity to distinguish yourself from other candidates. We have provided a sample thank you letter on the next page. Use this as a guideline to create your own personal thank you letter.

POWERHOUSE POINTER: Once you have written your thank you letter, let people you trust critique it. It is always good to get outside opinions and advice.

Sample Thank You Letter

(Name)
(Address) • (City, State Zip)
(Email address) • (Phone number)
(Date)
(Name)
(Title)
(Organization Name)
(Organization Address)
(City, State Zip)

Dear (Name):

I would like to thank you for taking time today to discuss the marketing position within your organization. Following our conversation about this opportunity, I feel more confident then ever that I would be a great fit for this position.

Furthermore, I believe that my experience and qualifications *(include items that were discussed during the interview),* including my proven track record, my creative marketing capabilities, and my customer service skills will all contribute to the achievements I would attain as part of your dynamic team.

As we discussed in our conversations today, there is an incredible amount of opportunity and growth in this market, and I feel confident that I can contribute to the success and the development of (Company).

Best regards,
(Name)
Enclosure

Ongoing Notes to Make You an Expert at Interviewing